GOING BEYOND
AMEN

Unveiling the Transformative Power of Prayer

ALISA L. GRACE

© 2024 Alisa L. Grace
All rights reserved.

No part of this book may be reproduced in any form or by any electronic or mechanical means, including information storage and retrieval systems, without permission in writing from the publisher.

Self-Published by
Alisa L. Grace
Sanford, FL 32771

ISBN: 978-1-966129-26-4

First Edition

Printed in the United States of America

Library of Congress Cataloging-in-Publication Data
Grace, Alisa L.

Title of the Book: Going Beyond Amen: Unveiling the Transformative Power of Prayer

Library of Congress Control Number: 2024925011

Disclaimer: The views expressed in this book are those of the author and do not necessarily reflect any organizations or individuals mentioned.

Acknowledgments: The author wishes to thank God, Her Husband (Linion), Victory Temple of God, Florida SPECS, Unity Youth Association, All About Serving You, Angels-ANJ Events, NordeVest, and Love & Create Life for their support and contributions.

Why Read This Book? - A Self-Discovery Survey

Are you ready to experience a deeper, more fulfilling prayer life? Take this quick survey to see if "Going Beyond Amen" is the right book for you:

- Do you often feel like your prayers are just words, lacking a true connection with God?
- Are you tired of unanswered prayers and wondering if you're doing something wrong?
- Do you long for a more intimate and dynamic relationship with your Heavenly Father?
- Are you seeking practical guidance on cultivating a consistent and effective prayer life?
- Do you want to experience the transformative power of prayer in your individual life, family, church, and even your business?
- Are you ready to embrace the challenge of surrendering your will to God and following His Word?

If you answered "yes" to any of these questions, then "Going Beyond Amen" is the book for you.'

This book is dedicated to the advancement of God's Kingdom. Through prayer, lives may be transformed, and His will be done on earth as it is in heaven.

In this book, you'll discover:

- The profound wisdom hidden within the Model Prayer
- Practical steps to cultivate an individual prayer life that honors God
- The vital role of prayer in strengthening the Church, families, and businesses
- The undeniable connection between obedience and answered prayer
- How to unlock a life of purpose and power through prayer

"Going Beyond Amen" is not just a book about prayer; it's a transformation journey. It calls for readers to embrace a deeper, more intimate relationship with God and experience the fullness of His blessings in every area of life.

Are you ready to go beyond "amen" and unlock the transformative power of prayer?

Table of Contents

Book Overview 1

Introduction 4

Part 1: The Model Prayer: Unlocking a Deeper Connection 7

Part 2: Cultivating an Individual Prayer Life that Honors God: A Transformative Journey 10

Part 3: The Family That Prays Together Stays Together: Building a Fortress of Faith 19

Part 4: The Business That Prays Together Stays Together: Thriving in Faith 23

Part 5: The Church That Prays Together Stays Together: Igniting Revival 27

30-Day Prayer Challenge: Transforming Lives Through Prayer 34

Individual Prayer Challenge 34

Family 30-Day Prayer Challenge 36

Church 30-Day Prayer Challenge 40

Thank You, and Keep Going, Prayer Warrior! 43

Don't Forget Your Companion! 44

Meet The Author: Alisa Ladawn Grace 45

Book Overview

Unveiling the Way of Life - A Transformative Journey into Prayer

- Prayer: A Universal Language
- Beyond Unanswered Prayers
- Embrace the Challenge
- Come, let's walk this transformative path together

Part 1: The Model Prayer - Unlocking a Deeper Connection

- A Prayer Centered on God
- Transformative Questions
- Prayer as a Way of Life

Part 2: Cultivating an Individual Prayer Life that Honors God - A Transformative Journey

- The Power of Surrender - Laying Down Our Agendas
- The Importance of Obedience - Aligning with His Word
- The Discipline of Daily Devotion - Nurturing the Connection

Part 3: The Family That Prays Together, Stays Together - Building a Fortress of Faith

- The Biblical Foundation: A Legacy of Prayer

- The Power of Unity: Strengthening Family Bonds
- The Protection of Prayer: Shielding Against Spiritual Attacks
- Embrace the Transformation

Part 4: The Business That Prays Together, Stays Together - Thriving in Faith

- The Biblical Mandate: Work as Worship
- The Power of Shared Vision: Uniting in Purpose
- The Provision of Prayer: Seeking God's Guidance
- Embrace the Transformation

Part 5: The Church That Prays Together, Stays Together - Igniting Revival

- The Biblical Foundation: A Praying Church
- The Power of Unity: Breaking Down Barriers
- The Presence of God: Igniting Revival
- Embrace the Transformation

Conclusion: Embracing Prayer as a Way of Life

- A Call to Action

30-Day Prayer Challenge: Transforming Lives Through Prayer

- Individual Prayer Challenge
- Family Prayer Challenge
- Business Prayer Challenge
- Church Prayer Challenge

Unlock Deeper Transformation with the "Going Beyond Amen" Journal Companions

Enhance your "Going Beyond Amen" experience with our companion journals, specifically designed for individuals, families, businesses, and churches. These journals provide a structured framework for daily reflection, prayer, and Scripture meditation, deepening your engagement with the 30-day challenge.

Each journal features:

- Daily entries with dedicated space for recording prayers, reflections, and gratitude lists.
- Thought-provoking questions aligned with each day's theme and Scripture.
- Ample space for personalizing your journey with notes, insights, and creative expression.

Choose the journal that best suits your needs:

- Individual Journal: Deepen your personal connection with God and experience individual transformation.
- Family Journal: Strengthen your family bond and build a lasting spiritual legacy together.
- Business Journal: Integrate faith into your workplace and experience God's guidance and provision in your business.
- Church Journal: Unite your congregation in prayer and ignite a revival of faith within your community.

Take your prayer journey to the next level with these influential companion journals!

Introduction

Why Praying Right is Essential: Unlocking the Power of True Connection

Prayer isn't just a spiritual practice for Christians; it's the lifeline connecting us to our Creator. Without it, our faith becomes a hollow performance devoid of the vibrant relationship God desires for us.

Imagine a bird without wings or a fish without gills—that's life without prayer.

Yet, countless prayers go unanswered, leaving many feeling discouraged and disconnected. We've all experienced the frustration of praying and waiting, only to be met with silence. We tell ourselves it's not God's will, but deep down, we wonder if we're doing something wrong.

What if the answer lies not in our requests but in our approach to prayer?

We've been taught to pray as a transaction—present our requests, say "amen," and expect results. But God has revealed a more profound truth: prayer isn't about making demands; it's a way of life.

Embark on a Transformative Journey

In this book, we'll guide you beyond the performance of prayer and into a life infused with its power. You'll learn:

- The true essence of prayer as revealed in the Model Prayer
- How to cultivate an individual prayer life that honors God
- The vital role of prayer in strengthening the Church, families, and businesses
- The profound connection between obedience and answered prayer

Get ready to revolutionize your prayer life. Discover how to cultivate a deep, abiding connection with God and experience the joy of answered prayers rooted in a relationship of love and obedience.

Prayer: Unveiling the Way of Life

Have you ever considered that prayer could be more than a sacred ritual or a performance? What if it's an intimate, dynamic way of life? God is revealing the true essence of prayer, and we're here to share this profound revelation with you.

Prayer: A Universal Language

Prayer, a universal language, resonates within the hearts of countless faiths worldwide. Let's briefly explore its significance within three major monotheistic religions:

1. **Islam:** Muslims offer prayers to Allah five times a day, weaving prayer into the fabric of their daily lives.

2. **Judaism:** Jews connect with the God of Abraham, Isaac, and Jacob through prayer three times daily, honoring their ancestral heritage.

3. **Christianity:** Christians, like the Jews, commune with the same God, Jesus, His Son, and the Holy Spirit. But for Christians, it's not just about establishing a connection; it's about nurturing a personal relationship through prayer.

While these religions offer rich prayer traditions, we focus on illuminating prayer from a Christian perspective, drawing from over 50 years of personal experience.

Beyond Unanswered Prayers

For years, unanswered prayers led to discouragement and a spiritual disconnect. We've all been there, crying out with fervent pleas, only to be silent. We settled for the notion that "it wasn't God's will," attending church out of tradition rather than a vibrant connection.

But God, in His infinite grace, led us to a transformative truth: a consistent, daily holy life is the key to unlocking the power of prayer. It's about seeking Him in designated services and every moment of our lives.

Part 1

The Model Prayer: Unlocking a Deeper Connection

Do you find yourself merely reciting prayers from a book, following a familiar ritual? Do you wonder why many of your prayers go unanswered? Let's dive deeper into the heart of prayer, exploring the profound wisdom within the Model Prayer found in Matthew 6:9-13:

Our Father in heaven, Hallowed be Your name. Your kingdom come. Your will be done On earth, as it is in heaven. Give us this day our daily bread. And forgive us our debts. As we forgive our debtors. And do not lead us into temptation, But deliver us from the evil one. For Yours is the kingdom and the power and the glory forever. Amen.

For many of us, this prayer has been a lifelong companion. But what if we allowed Christ Himself to teach us how to pray through these words instead of mere repetition?

A Prayer Centered on God

Notice how the entire prayer revolves around God. It's a model of approaching the throne of grace, not with our agenda but with a heart surrendered to His will.

"Our Father in heaven, Hallowed be Your name."
We enter God's presence with humility, acknowledging Him as our Father, worthy of all honor and reverence. For too long, many

of us have approached prayer with a "me-centered" focus, seeking God's blessings for our own plans and desires. But true prayer begins with adoration, recognizing His sovereignty, and shifting our focus from ourselves to Him.

Transformative Question #1: *How can I shift my focus in prayer from my own needs and desires to honoring and adoring God?*

"Your kingdom come. Your will be done On earth, as it is in heaven."

This isn't about getting God's stamp of approval on our own agenda. It's about aligning our hearts with His Kingdom—seeking His will above our own and desiring to see His purposes fulfilled in our lives and the world around us. This requires a deep surrender, allowing the Holy Spirit to guide our thoughts, desires, and actions.

Transformative Question #2: *Am I truly seeking God's will above my own, or am I simply asking Him to bless my own plans?*

"Give us this day our daily bread."

In a world consumed by greed and the pursuit of more, this simple request reminds us to trust God for our daily needs. It's a call to contentment, recognizing that true provision comes from Him, not from our striving or accumulation of possessions.

Transformative Question #3: *How can I cultivate a heart of contentment, trusting God to provide for my daily needs?*

"And forgive us our debts, As we forgive our debtors."

Forgiveness lies at the heart of our relationship with God and with others. We acknowledge our need for forgiveness while extending that grace to those who wronged us. Unforgiveness creates a barrier between us and God, hindering our prayers and stunting our spiritual growth.

"And do not lead us into temptation, But deliver us from the evil one. For Yours is the kingdom and the power and the glory forever. Amen."

We recognize our own weakness and dependence on God's strength to resist temptation and overcome evil. We acknowledge His ultimate authority and give Him all the glory.

Prayer as a Way of Life

The Model Prayer isn't just a set of words to be recited; it's a blueprint for a life lived in constant communion with God. As 1 Thessalonians 5:17 reminds us, we must "pray without ceasing." This means cultivating an ongoing conversation with our Heavenly Father, seeking His guidance, expressing our gratitude, and aligning our hearts with His will in every moment.

Let's move beyond the performance of prayer and embrace it as the vibrant, life-giving connection it was meant to be.

Part 2

Cultivating an Individual Prayer Life that Honors God: A Transformative Journey

Are you tired of prayers that feel empty and unanswered? Prepare to embark on a transformative journey where prayer becomes more than a routine – a vibrant, life-giving connection with God.

In the following sections, we'll uncover the secrets to cultivating an individual prayer life that truly honors Him. Discover the power of surrendering your will, the undeniable link between obedience, answered prayer, and daily devotion's transformative discipline. Get ready to experience a profound shift in your prayer life as you enter a deeper, more intimate relationship with your Heavenly Father.

This section delves into the heart of cultivating an individual prayer life that truly honors God. We'll explore:

1. **The Power of Surrender:** True prayer begins with a surrendered heart that seeks God's will above all else. It's about laying down our agendas and desires and embracing His plans for our lives.

2. **The Importance of Obedience:** Answered prayers aren't a matter of luck or chance; they're directly tied to our obedience to God's Word. When we align our lives with His commands, we open the door for Him to move mightily on our behalf.

3. **The Discipline of Daily Devotion:** A consistent prayer life requires discipline and intentionality. It's about setting aside

time daily to connect with God, listen to His voice, and seek His guidance.

Transformative Questions:

As you embark on this journey, consider these questions:

- **Am I truly surrendered to God's will, or am I still clinging to my own plans and desires?**
- **Am I living in obedience to God's Word, or am I picking and choosing which commands to follow?**
- **Am I making time for daily prayer and devotion, or am I allowing other things to crowd out my time with God?**

These questions will challenge you to examine your heart and prayer life. They will invite you to step out of your comfort zone and embrace a deeper, more intimate relationship with God.

Remember, prayer isn't about getting what we want; it's about aligning our hearts with God's. It's about surrendering our will to His and trusting Him to lead us on the path He has prepared for us. As you cultivate a prayer life that honors God, you'll experience a transformation beyond answered prayers. You'll discover a more profound sense of peace, joy, and purpose as you walk hand-in-hand with your Heavenly Father.

So, let's embark on this journey together. Let's learn to pray not just with our lips but with our hearts, minds, and souls. Let's cultivate a prayer life that honors God and brings His Kingdom to earth.

The Power of Surrender - Laying Down Our Agendas

In the tapestry of a vibrant prayer life, surrender is the golden thread that weaves everything together. It's the profound act of laying down our agendas, desires, and plans at God's feet, recognizing His ultimate sovereignty, and embracing His perfect will for our lives.

Jesus, our ultimate example, demonstrated this surrender beautifully in the Garden of Gethsemane. In the face of immense suffering, He prayed, "Father, if you are willing, take this cup from me; yet not my will, but yours be done" (Luke 22:42). Even in His humanity, Jesus chose to align His will with the Father's, trusting in His divine plan.

Surrender isn't about passivity or resignation. It's an active choice to relinquish control, to acknowledge that God's ways are higher than our own (Isaiah 55:9). It's a recognition that His wisdom surpasses our understanding, and His love for us is unfailing.

Embracing the Paradox of Surrender

Surrender, in its essence, is a paradox. It's in letting go that we find true freedom. It's in yielding our will that we discover God's perfect plan. In dying to self, we experience the fullness of life in Christ.

As Paul writes in Galatians 2:20, "I have been crucified with Christ, and I no longer live, but Christ lives in me. The life I now live in the body, I live by faith in the Son of God, who loved me and gave himself for me."

Practical Steps to Surrender

While surrender is a profound spiritual act, it also requires practical implementation in our daily lives. Here are a few steps to help you cultivate a heart of surrender:

1. **Start with Confession:** Acknowledge any areas where you've been clinging to your own desires or plans. Confess these to God, asking for His forgiveness and help to release them.

2. **Practice Daily Surrender:** Make it a habit to surrender your day to God each morning. Invite Him to guide your steps, decisions, and interactions. Pray, "Lord, today I surrender my will to yours. May your purposes be fulfilled in and through me."

3. **Embrace His Leading:** Be open to God's redirection, even if it means letting go of something you've been holding onto tightly. Trust that He leads you towards a greater good, even when the path seems uncertain.

4. **Seek His Wisdom:** When faced with decisions, seek God's wisdom through prayer and studying His Word. Ask Him to reveal His will and give you the strength to follow it.

5. **Cultivate Gratitude:** Thank God for His sovereignty and perfect plan for your life. Express gratitude for His guidance and provision, even amid challenges.

Remember, surrender is an ongoing process, not a one-time event. It requires daily recommitment and a willingness to let go of our own agendas. But as we surrender to God's will, we open ourselves to the fullness of His blessings and experience the true freedom that comes from living in alignment with His purposes.

The Importance of Obedience - Aligning with His Word

Imagine a dance where two partners move in perfect harmony, their steps synchronized, their hearts intertwined. This beautiful picture reflects the essence of a prayer life rooted in obedience. Jesus, our loving Savior, invites us into this divine dance when He says, "If you love me, keep my commands" (John 14:15).

Obedience is not a burden or a legalistic checklist; it expresses our love for God and is a key to unlocking the power of prayer. When we align our lives with His Word, we position ourselves to receive His blessings and experience the fullness of His promises.

The Connection Between Obedience and Answered Prayer

In 1 John 3:22, we read, "And whatever we ask we receive from him because we keep his commands and do what pleases him." This verse reveals a profound truth: obedience paves the way for answered prayer. When we live by God's will, our prayers are in harmony with His purposes, and He delights to answer them.

Furthermore, Jesus Himself emphasizes the importance of obedience in John 15:7: "If you remain in me and my words remain in you, ask whatever you wish, and it will be done for you." When we abide in Christ and His Word, our desires align with His, and our prayers become powerful and effective.

Practical Steps to Obedience

Obedience is not a passive concept; it requires intentional action and a willingness to submit our will to God. Here are some practical steps to help you cultivate a life of obedience:

1. **Study the Bible:** Immerse yourself in God's Word; it will shape your thoughts, beliefs, and actions. Make Bible reading and study a daily priority, seeking to understand His commands and apply them to your life.

2. **Apply His Commands:** Don't just read the Bible; put its teachings into practice in your daily life. Seek opportunities to demonstrate your love for God through acts of big and small obedience.

3. **Confess and Repent:** When you fall short, be quick to confess your sins and seek God's forgiveness. 1 John 1:9 assures us "that when we confess our sins, he is faithful and just and will forgive us our sins and purify us from all unrighteousness." Repentance is not just about feeling sorry; it's about turning away from sin and turning back toward God.

4. **Seek Accountability:** Surround yourself with other believers who can encourage you in your walk with God and hold you accountable to His Word. Share your struggles and victories with them, and pray for one another.

5. **Cultivate a Teachable Spirit:** Be open to correction and instruction from the Holy Spirit and other mature believers. Recognize that growth in obedience is a lifelong process.

Remember, obedience is not about earning God's favor but responding to His love. As we align our lives with His Word, we experience the joy of answered prayer, the peace of His presence, and the fullness of His blessings.

The Discipline of Daily Devotion - Nurturing the Connection

Imagine a friendship in which you only spoke to your friend once a week or during emergencies. Would that relationship flourish? Hardly. Just as any meaningful relationship thrives on consistent communication, so does our relationship with God. A vibrant prayer life requires dedicated time daily to connect with Him, listen to His voice, and pour out your heart.

The Bible frequently reminds us to seek God diligently. In Jeremiah 29:13, He says, "You will seek me and find me when you seek me with all your heart." Seeking Him requires an active pursuit, a daily commitment to spending time in His presence.

Jesus, our perfect example, often withdrew to solitary places to pray (Luke 5:16). He understood the importance of prioritizing time with His Father, even amidst a busy ministry.

Practical Steps to Cultivate Daily Devotion

While daily devotion may seem daunting, it's about fostering a consistent connection, not achieving perfection. Here are some practical steps to help you nurture this vital discipline:

1. **Find a Quiet Place:** Designate a distraction-free space where you can focus solely on God. This could be a cozy corner in your home, a peaceful outdoor setting, or even a quiet chapel.

You must minimize distractions and create an atmosphere conducive to prayer and reflection.

2. **Set a Regular Time:** Establish a consistent prayer routine that fits your schedule. Whether it's early morning, during your lunch break, or before bed, choose when you can be most alert and focused. Consistency is vital to building a sustainable habit.

3. **Use Various Prayer Methods:** Incorporate different forms of prayer into your daily devotion. Adoration involves praising God for who He is. Confession involves acknowledging your shortcomings and seeking His forgiveness. Thanksgiving consists in expressing gratitude for His blessings. Supplication involves presenting your requests to Him.

4. **Engage with Scripture:** Read and meditate on God's Word, allowing it to speak to your heart and guide your prayers. The Bible is a treasure box full of wisdom, promises, and encouragement.

5. **Journal Your Prayers:** Writing down your prayers can help you track your conversations with God, reflect on His answers, and identify growth areas in your prayer life.

6. **Listen for His Voice:** As you pray, be still and listen for God's gentle whispers. He may speak through Scripture, a quiet thought, or a circumstance. Be attentive to His leading and guidance.

Remember, daily devotion is not about fulfilling a religious obligation but nurturing a loving relationship with your Heavenly Father. As you prioritize time with Him, you'll experience a profound shift in your spiritual life. As you walk hand-in-hand with the One who loves you most, you'll discover a more profound sense of peace, joy, and purpose.

Embrace the Transformation

Cultivating a consistent prayer life has its challenges. There will be days when distractions abound and motivation wanes. But as you persevere, you'll witness the transformative power of prayer in your own life.

You'll find that your heart becomes more attuned to God's will, your faith grows more robust, and your relationship with Him deepens. You'll experience the joy of answered prayers, the comfort of His presence, and the confidence from knowing you're walking in His perfect plan.

So, let's commit to prioritizing daily devotion. Let's set aside time each day to connect with our Heavenly Father, to listen to His voice, and to pour out our hearts. As we nurture this vital connection, we'll experience the abundant life He desires for us, a life overflowing with His love, peace, and joy.

Part 3

The Family That Prays Together Stays Together: Building a Fortress of Faith

In a world where families are crumbling under the weight of busyness, distractions, and societal pressures, could the simple act of praying together be the key to strengthening the bonds that hold us dear? What if the family unit, designed by God to be a haven of love and support, could become an unbreakable fortress of faith through the power of prayer?

In this chapter, we explore the transformative impact of family prayer. We'll delve into:

1. **The Biblical Foundation:** Discover the scriptural basis for family prayer and its role in God's plan.

2. **The Power of Unity:** Witness how praying together fosters unity, strengthens relationships, and creates a shared spiritual legacy.

3. **The Protection of Prayer:** Learn how family prayer shields against spiritual attacks, provides guidance and cultivates a godly heritage.

Transformative Questions:

As you embark on this journey of family prayer, consider these questions:

1. Are we prioritizing prayer as a family, or are we allowing the busyness of life to overshadow our spiritual connection?
2. Are we actively seeking God's guidance and protection for our family through prayer, or are we relying solely on our own strength?
3. Are we creating a legacy of faith for future generations through our commitment to family prayer?

These questions challenge us to examine the role of prayer in our families and to embrace its transformative power.

The Biblical Foundation: A Legacy of Prayer

Throughout Scripture, we witness the profound impact of family prayer. From Abraham, who built altars and called on the name of the Lord with his family (Genesis 12:8), to Joshua, who declared, "As for me and my house, we will serve the Lord" (Joshua 24:15), the Bible paints a picture of families united in their pursuit of God.

In the New Testament, Jesus is praying with His disciples, modeling the importance of shared prayer and spiritual connection. Paul also encourages families to pray together, writing in Ephesians 6:18, "And pray in the Spirit on all occasions with all kinds of prayers and requests. With this in mind, be alert and always pray for all the Lord's people."

The Power of Unity: Strengthening Family Bonds

When families pray together, they create a powerful bond that overpowers the challenges of everyday life. Shared prayer fosters unity, deepens relationships, and makes a shared spiritual legacy.

Psalm 133:1 beautifully states, "How good and pleasant it is when God's people live together in unity!" Family prayer cultivates this unity, reminding us that we are all part of something bigger than ourselves—we are a part of God's family.

Praying together also strengthens individual relationships within the family. When parents pray with their children, it creates a safe space for open and honest communication, vulnerability, and shared faith. It models the importance of seeking God's guidance and relying on His strength.

Moreover, family prayer establishes a spiritual legacy that can be passed down through generations. Children witnessing their parents prioritizing prayer instill a deep reverence for God and a desire to seek Him throughout their lives.

The Protection of Prayer: Shielding Against Spiritual Attacks

In a world filled with spiritual battles, family prayer is a powerful shield of protection. When we pray together, we invite God's presence into our homes, creating a barrier against the enemy's schemes.

Ephesians 6:10-12 reminds us, "Finally, be strong in the Lord and in his gracious and mighty power. Be sure to put on the full armor of God so that you can stand against the devil's schemes. For our struggle is not against our flesh and blood, but against the rulers, against the authorities, against the powers of this wicked world, and against the spiritual forces of evil in the heavenly realms."

Family prayer equips us with the spiritual armor to withstand these attacks. It empowers us to stand firm in our faith, resist temptation, and overcome the challenges that come our way.

Furthermore, praying together provides guidance and discernment for families. As we seek God's wisdom through prayer, He illuminates our path, helping us make decisions that honor Him and lead to His blessings.

Embrace the Transformation

As you prioritize family prayer, you'll witness its transformative power in your home. Relationships will deepen, faith will flourish, and a legacy of godliness will be established. You'll experience the joy of walking together in God's purposes, united in His love and strengthened by His grace.

So, let's commit to making family prayer a priority. Let's gather regularly, lift our voices in unity, and seek God's guidance for our lives. As we do, we'll create a fortress of faith that will stand strong against any storm.

Part 4

The Business That Prays Together Stays Together: Thriving in Faith

In a world where businesses crumble under the weight of competition, economic downturns, and ethical compromises, could the simple act of praying together be the key to unlocking a new level of success? What if the workplace, often seen as a battleground for profit and power, could become a sanctuary of shared faith and purpose?

In this chapter, we explore the transformative impact of prayer in the business world. We'll delve into:

1. **The Biblical Mandate:** Uncover the scriptural principles that support prayer in the workplace and its role in God's plan for our work.

2. **The Power of Shared Vision:** Witness how praying together fosters unity, aligns goals, and creates a culture of integrity and excellence.

3. **The Provision of Prayer:** Learn how seeking God's guidance in business leads to wisdom, provision, and ethical decision-making.

Transformative Questions:

As you consider incorporating prayer into your business, ponder these questions:
1. Are we acknowledging God's sovereignty over our business or relying solely on our own abilities and strategies?

2. Are we seeking His guidance in our decision-making, or are we driven solely by profit and competition?

3. Are we creating a workplace culture that reflects His values of integrity, compassion, and excellence?

These questions challenge us to reimagine the role of faith in our businesses and to embrace the transformative power of prayer.

The Biblical Mandate: Work as Worship

The Bible views work not merely as a means to an end but as an act of worship. Colossians 3:23-24 reminds us, "Whatever you do, work at it with all your heart, as working for the Lord, not for human masters, since you know you will receive an inheritance from the Lord as a reward. It is the Lord Christ you are serving."

When we approach our work with this perspective, we recognize that God is intimately involved in every aspect of our business. Prayer becomes a natural extension of this understanding as we seek His guidance, wisdom, and provision.

Proverbs 3:5-6 encourages us, "Trust in the Lord with all your heart and lean not on your own understanding; in all your ways submit to him, and he will make your paths straight." By incorporating prayer into our business practices, we acknowledge our dependence on God and invite Him to direct our steps.

The Power of Shared Vision: Uniting in Purpose

When a business prays together, it creates a shared vision and purpose that transcends individual goals. It fosters unity among employees, aligns their efforts, and cultivates a culture of integrity and excellence.

Matthew 18:19-20 promises, "Again, truly I tell you that if two of you on earth agree about anything they ask for, it will be done for them by my Father in heaven. For where two or three gather in my name, there am I with them." This powerful principle applies not only to personal prayer but also to the workplace.

When colleagues gather in prayer, seeking God's guidance and blessing for their business, they create an atmosphere where His presence is felt and His power is unleashed. It fosters a sense of teamwork, mutual support, and shared accountability.

Moreover, praying together encourages ethical decision-making and a commitment to integrity. As we seek God's wisdom, we are less likely to compromise our values or engage in practices that dishonor Him.

The Provision of Prayer: Seeking God's Guidance

Prayer is not just about asking God for blessings; it's also about seeking His guidance and wisdom in every aspect of our business. When we invite Him into our decision-making processes, we tap into a source of infinite wisdom and understanding.

James 1:5 reminds us, "If any of you lacks wisdom, you should ask God, who gives generously to all without finding fault, and it will be given to you." Whether facing a challenging negotiation, a difficult staffing decision, or a financial crisis, prayer provides a lifeline to God's wisdom and provision.

Furthermore, prayer helps us cultivate a spirit of gratitude and contentment, even during challenges. We trust His faithfulness more as we acknowledge God's blessings and provision.

Embrace the Transformation

As you incorporate prayer into your business, you'll witness its transformative power. Your workplace will become a place of shared purpose, ethical decision-making, and God's abundant blessings. You'll experience the joy of working together in unity, guided by His wisdom and fueled by His strength.

So, let's commit to making prayer integral to our business practices. Let's gather together regularly, seeking God's guidance and blessing for our work. As we do, we'll create a workplace culture reflecting His values, experiences, and abundant provision.

Part 5

The Church That Prays Together Stays Together: Igniting Revival

In a world where churches struggle to maintain their relevance and impact, could the simple act of praying together be the key to unlocking a new era of spiritual vitality? What if the church, often seen as a social club or a platform for personal agendas, could become a powerhouse of prayer, fueled by unity and empowered by the Holy Spirit?

In this chapter, we explore the transformative impact of prayer within the church. We'll delve into:

1. **The Biblical Foundation:** Uncover the scriptural mandate for corporate prayer and its role in the early church's life.

2. **The Power of Unity:** Witness how praying together fosters unity, breaks down barriers, and creates a community of believers empowered for God's purposes.

3. **The Presence of God:** Learn how corporate prayer invites the Holy Spirit's presence, leading to revival, transformation, and spiritual breakthroughs.

Transformative Questions:

As you consider the role of prayer in your church, ponder these questions:

1. Are we prioritizing prayer as a church body or allowing programs and activities to overshadow our dependence on God?

2. Are we actively seeking God's guidance and direction through corporate prayer or relying solely on human wisdom and strategies?

3. Are we creating an atmosphere where the Holy Spirit can move freely, leading to revival and transformation in our midst?

These questions challenge us to reimagine the role of prayer in our churches and to embrace its transformative power.

The Biblical Foundation: A Praying Church

A genuine commitment to prayer marked the early church; in Acts 2:42, we read, "They devoted themselves to the apostles' teaching and fellowship, to the breaking of bread and prayer." Prayer was not an afterthought or an optional activity; it was the lifeblood of their community.

In Acts 4:31, we witness the power of corporate prayer: "After they prayed, the place where they were meeting was shaken. And they were all filled with the Holy Spirit and spoke the word of God boldly." Their unified prayers ushered in the presence of the Holy Spirit, empowering them to fulfill their mission.

Throughout the New Testament, we see numerous examples of the early church gathering to pray, seeking God's guidance, strength, and provision. Their commitment to prayer laid the foundation for the church's explosive growth and impact.

The Power of Unity: Breaking Down Barriers

When a church prays together, it creates powerful unity and connection. It breaks down barriers, fosters reconciliation, and empowers a community of believers for God's purposes.

Jesus Himself prayed for unity among His followers, saying in John 17:20-21, "My prayer is not for them alone. I pray also for those who will believe in me through their message, that all of them may be one, Father, just as you are in me and I am in you. May they also be in us so the world may believe you have sent me."

Corporate prayer cultivates this unity, reminding us that we are all part of the body of Christ, interconnected and interdependent. It fosters a sense of belonging, mutual support, and shared responsibility.

Moreover, praying together creates an atmosphere of vulnerability and authenticity. As we share our burdens, confess our sins, and praise God, we experience a deeper level of connection with one another.

The Presence of God: Igniting Revival

When a church gathers in prayer, it invites the Holy Spirit to move in its midst. This can lead to revival, transformation, and spiritual breakthroughs.

In 2 Chronicles 7:14, God promises, "If my people, who are called by my name, will humble themselves and pray and seek my face and turn from their wicked ways, then I will hear from heaven, and I will forgive their sin and will heal their land."

Corporate prayer creates an atmosphere of humility, repentance, and seeking God's face. It opens the door for His presence to fill the church, bringing healing, restoration, and renewal.

Furthermore, praying together empowers the church to fulfill its mission. As we seek God's guidance and direction, He equips us with the wisdom, courage, and resources we need to impact our communities and advance His Kingdom.

Embrace the Transformation

As you prioritize corporate prayer in your church, you'll witness its transformative power. Barriers will crumble, relationships will deepen, and the Holy Spirit will move in unprecedented ways. You'll experience the joy of walking together in unity, empowered by God's presence and fulfilling His purposes.

So, let's commit to making prayer a central focus of our church life. Let's gather regularly, lift our voices in unity, and seek God's guidance for our congregation. As we do, we'll create a spiritual powerhouse that shines brightly in a dark world.

Conclusion: Embracing Prayer as a Way of Life

As we conclude this transformative journey, let us reflect on the profound truths we have discovered about prayer's power and purpose.
We began by exploring the Model Prayer, a timeless blueprint for approaching God with reverence, surrender, and a focus on His Kingdom. We learned that prayer is not about presenting a wish list to a cosmic genie but about aligning our hearts with God's will and seeking His purposes above our own.

We then delved into cultivating an individual prayer life that honors God. We discovered that true prayer flows from a heart surrendered to His will, a life lived in obedience to His Word, and a commitment to daily devotion.

We also explored the vital role of prayer in strengthening the Church, families, and businesses. We saw how praying together fosters unity, breaks down barriers, and creates a powerful force for God's Kingdom. We witnessed how family prayer builds a fortress of faith, protects against spiritual attacks, and establishes a godly legacy. We also learned how prayer in the workplace can transform businesses into thriving communities of shared purpose and ethical practices.

Throughout this journey, we have seen the undeniable connection between obedience and answered prayer. When we align our lives with God's commands, we open the door for Him to move mightily on our behalf.

A Call to Action

Now, dear reader, it's time to put these truths into practice. Embrace prayer not as a religious duty but as a vibrant, life-giving connection with your Heavenly Father.

1. **Surrender your will to His:** Let go of your own agendas and desires and trust in His perfect plan for your life.

2. **Live in obedience to His Word:** Study the Bible, apply its teachings, and seek to please Him in all you do.
3. **Cultivate a daily devotional life:** Set aside time each day to connect with God, to listen to His voice, and to pour out your heart.

Pray with your family and your church. As you lift your voices together in prayer, Experience the power of unity and shared faith. Invite God into your workplace: Seek His guidance and wisdom in every aspect of your business and create a culture of integrity and excellence.

As you embrace prayer as a way of life, you'll witness its transformative power in every area of your life. You'll experience more profound peace, greater joy, and a more fulfilling purpose. You'll see God move miraculously, answering your prayers and exceeding your expectations.

Remember, prayer is not a magic formula or a quick fix. It's a lifelong journey of deepening intimacy with God. It's about cultivating a relationship of trust, surrender, and obedience.

So, let's continue this journey together. Let's pray without ceasing, seeking God's face and walking in His will. As we do, we'll experience the abundant life He desires for us, a life overflowing with His love, peace, and joy.

30-Day Prayer Challenge: Transforming Lives Through Prayer

This 30-day prayer challenge is designed to help individuals, families, businesses, and churches deepen their connection with God and experience the transformative power of prayer. Each day focuses on a specific aspect of prayer, drawing inspiration from the key themes explored in this book.

Remember, this 30-day prayer challenge is just a starting point. As you continue to prioritize prayer in your individual life, family, business, and church, you'll experience its transformative power and see God work in incredible ways.

Individual Prayer Challenge

1. **Surrender:** Pray for a heart fully surrendered to God's will.
2. **Obedience:** Ask God to reveal any areas where you need to align your life with His Word.
3. **Daily Devotion:** Commit to spending dedicated time with God each day.
4. **Adoration:** Spend time praising God for His attributes and character.
5. **Confession:** Confess any sins or shortcomings and receive His forgiveness.
6. **Thanksgiving:** Express gratitude for God's blessings in your life.
7. Supplication: Present your requests to God with confidence and trust.
8. **Listening:** Be still and listen for God's voice through Scripture, thoughts, or circumstances.
9. **Forgiveness:** Forgive those who have wronged you, and ask God to help you release bitterness.

10. **Guidance:** Seek God's wisdom and direction for your life.
11. **Protection:** Pray for God's protection over you and your loved ones.
12. **Provision:** Trust God to provide for your physical and spiritual needs.
13. **Spiritual Growth:** Ask God to help you grow in your faith and knowledge of Him.
14. **Relationships:** Pray for healing and restoration in your relationships.
15. **Dreams and Goals:** Surrender your dreams and goals to God, seeking His will for your future.
16. **Rest:** Ask God to give you rest and peace in your soul.
17. **Strength:** Pray for strength to overcome challenges and temptations.
18. **Boldness:** Ask God to give you the boldness to share your faith with others.
19. **The Lost:** Pray for the salvation of those who don't know Jesus.
20. **The Church:** Pray for unity and revival in the global Church.
21. **Your Community:** Pray for God's blessings and transformation in your community.
22. **The Nations**: Pray for peace and justice throughout the world.
23. The Model Prayer: Meditate on the Lord's Prayer and pray it with understanding.
24. **Fasting:** Consider incorporating a partial or full fast to deepen your focus on God.
25. **Gratitude Journal:** Write down three things you're grateful for each day.
26. **Memorize Scripture**: Choose a verse or passage to memorize and meditate on.
27. **Pray with a Friend:** Share your prayer requests and pray together for each other.
28. **Serve Others:** Look for opportunities to serve others and show God's love in action.

29. **Worship:** Spend time praising God and expressing your love for Him.
30. **Reflection:** Review the past 30 days and thank God for His faithfulness.

Family 30-Day Prayer Challenge

1. **Unity:** Pray for unity and strong bonds within your family.
2. **Communication:** Ask God to help you communicate openly and honestly with each other.
3. **Forgiveness:** Forgive each other for any past hurts and seek reconciliation.
4. **Protection:** Pray for God's protection over your family from physical and spiritual harm.
5. **Guidance:** Seek God's wisdom and direction for your family's decisions.
6. **Provision:** Trust God to provide for your family's needs.
7. **Spiritual Growth:** Pray for each family member to grow in their faith.
8. **Relationships:** Pray for healthy relationships within your extended family.
9. **Children:** Pray for your children's salvation, protection, and guidance.
10. **Parents:** Pray for your parents' health, wisdom, and spiritual well-being.
11. **Marriage:** If applicable, pray for a strong and God-honoring marriage.
12. **Finances:** Seek God's wisdom in managing your family's finances.
13. **Home:** Pray for God's blessings and peace to fill your home.
14. **Education:** Pray for your children's education and future endeavors.
15. **Health:** Pray for your family's physical, emotional, and spiritual health.

16. **Gratitude:** Express gratitude for each family member and their unique gifts.
17. **Family Devotions:** Read the Bible and pray together as a family.
18. **Serve Together:** Find opportunities to serve others as a family.
19. **Legacy:** Pray for God to establish a legacy of faith in your family for generations.
20. **Celebration:** Celebrate God's faithfulness and answered prayers as a family.
21. **Community Impact:** Pray for God's blessings and transformation in your local community. Ask Him to guide your family in ways to serve and make a positive difference.
22. **Global Perspective:** Pray for peace and justice throughout the world. Lift up nations experiencing conflict, injustice, or natural disasters, and ask God to bring healing and restoration.
23. **The Model Prayer:** Meditate on the Lord's Prayer as a family. Discuss its meaning and pray it together with understanding.
24. **Fasting Together:** Consider incorporating a family fast, even just for a meal or a specific period. Use this time to focus on prayer and seek God's guidance.
25. **Family Gratitude Journal:** Each family member writes and shares three things they're grateful for during prayer time.
26. **Scripture Memory:** Choose a verse or passage to memorize and meditate on together as a family. Discuss its meaning and application to your lives.
27. **Pray with Another Family:** Invite another family over for a meal or fellowship, and spend time praying together for each other's needs and concerns.
28. **Family Service Project:** Find a local service opportunity your family can participate in together, demonstrating God's love in action.
29. **Family Worship Night:** Set aside an evening for family worship, singing praises to God, sharing testimonies, and expressing your love for Him.

30. **Reflection and Thanksgiving:** Look back on the past 30 days as a family. Share how you've seen God work, express gratitude for answered prayers, and celebrate His faithfulness.

Business 30- Day Prayer Challenge

1. **God's Ownership:** Acknowledge God's ownership and sovereignty over your business.
2. **Shared Vision:** Pray for unity and a shared vision among your team.
3. **Ethical Practices:** Seek God's guidance in making ethical and integrity-driven decisions.
4. **Wisdom:** Ask for wisdom in managing your business and overcoming challenges.
5. **Provision:** Trust God to provide for your business's needs and financial stability.
6. **Employee Well-being:** Pray for your employees' physical, emotional, and spiritual well-being.
7. **Customer Relationships:** Pray for positive and fruitful relationships with your customers.
8. **Growth:** Seek God's guidance for growth and expansion opportunities.
9. **Innovation:** Ask for creativity and innovation in your products or services.
10. **Influence:** Pray for your business to impact your community and industry positively.
11. **Workplace Culture:** Pray for a workplace culture that reflects God's values.
12. **Conflict Resolution:** Seek God's help in resolving conflicts and disagreements.
13. **Decision-Making:** Pray for discernment and wisdom when making important decisions.
14. **Gratitude:** Express gratitude for your business, team, and customers.

15. **Team Meetings:** Start or end your team meetings with prayer.
16. **Serve the Community:** Find ways for your business to serve and give back to the community.
17. **Testimonies:** Share stories of how God has answered prayers and worked in your business.
18. **Stewardship:** Pray for a spirit of stewardship and generosity in your business practices.
19. **God's Glory:** Dedicate your business to bringing glory to God.
20. **Celebration:** Celebrate milestones and achievements, acknowledging God's provision and guidance.
21. **Community Impact:** Pray for God's blessings and transformation in your local community. Seek ways your business can contribute positively and make a difference.
22. **Global Perspective:** Pray for peace and justice throughout the world. Consider how your business can support ethical practices and contribute to a better world.
23. **The Model Prayer:** Meditate on the Lord's Prayer as a team. Discuss its implications for your business, seeking to align your goals and practices with God's will.
24. **Team Fasting:** If appropriate for your team, consider a partial or complete fast together, dedicating the time to prayer and seeking God's guidance for the business.
25. **Gratitude Wall:** Create a space where employees can write down things they are grateful for in their work and personal lives.
26. **Scripture Focus:** Choose a verse or passage relevant to business or teamwork and encourage employees to memorize and reflect on it.
27. **Pray with a Partner Business:** Connect with another Christian-owned business and pray together for each other's ventures and challenges.
28. **Community Service Day:** Organize a team service project in your community to demonstrate your business's commitment to serving others.

29. **Workplace Worship:** Dedicate time during a lunch break or team meeting for worship, praise God, and express gratitude for His provision.
30. **Reflection and Celebration:** Gather as a team to reflect on the past 30 days. Share testimonies of answered prayers and celebrate God's faithfulness in your business journey.

Church 30-Day Prayer Challenge

1. **Revival:** Pray for a spiritual awakening and revival in your church.
2. **Unity:** Ask God to unite your church body in love and purpose.
3. **Leadership:** Pray for your pastors, elders, and leaders that they will be filled with wisdom and the Holy Spirit.
4. **Outreach:** Pray for effective outreach and evangelism in your community.
5. **Spiritual Growth:** Pray for each church member to grow in their faith and relationship with God.
6. **Discipleship:** Pray for strong discipleship programs and opportunities for spiritual mentorship.
7. **Worship:** Pray for powerful and Spirit-filled worship services.
8. **Prayer Meetings:** Commit to attending and actively participating in your church's prayer meetings.
9. **Missions:** Pray for missionaries and their work around the world.
10. **Healing:** Pray for physical, emotional, and spiritual healing for those in your church and community.
11. **Deliverance:** Pray for freedom from spiritual bondage and oppression.
12. **Financial Provision:** Pray for God's provision for your church's needs and ministries.
13. **Facilities:** Pray for God's blessing on your church building and facilities.
14. **Children and Youth:** Pray for the spiritual growth and

protection of the young people in your church.
15. **Families:** Pray for strong and God-honoring families within your church.
16. **Gratitude:** Express gratitude for your church family and all that God is doing.
17. **Prayer Walks:** Organize prayer walks in your community, praying for specific needs and areas.
18. **Serve Together:** Find opportunities for your church to serve the community together.
19. **Global Impact:** Pray for your church to impact God's Kingdom globally.
20. **Celebration:** Celebrate answered prayers and God's faithfulness in your church.
21. **Community Outreach:** Pray for God's blessings and transformation in your local community. Seek ways your church can actively serve and make a positive impact.
22. **Global Vision:** Pray for peace and justice throughout the world. Lift up nations experiencing conflict, injustice, or natural disasters, and ask God to bring healing and restoration.
23. **The Model Prayer in Community:** Gather as a church body to meditate on the Lord's Prayer. Discuss its implications for your congregation and pray it together with understanding.
24. **Corporate Fast:** Encourage members to consider a partial or complete fast, dedicating the time to seeking God's face and direction for the church.
25. **Gratitude Wall:** Create a designated space in the church where members can write down their praises and thanksgiving.
26. **Scripture Memory Challenge:** Choose a verse or passage as a church to memorize and meditate on together. Encourage members to share insights and applications during small group or prayer meetings.
27. **Prayer Partners:** Pair up church members to pray for each other regularly, fostering deeper connections and accountability within the body.

28. **Community Service Day:** Organize a church-wide service project that demonstrates God's love in action and meets tangible needs in your community.
29. **Night of Worship and Prayer:** Host a special evening dedicated to worship and prayer, creating space for heartfelt expressions of love and surrender to God.
30. **Testimony & Thanksgiving Service:** Conclude the challenge with a service focused on sharing testimonies of answered prayers and expressing gratitude for God's faithfulness throughout the 30 days.

Thank You, and Keep Going, Prayer Warrior!

Dear Prayer Warrior,

Congratulations on taking the first step in your Going Beyond Amen journey! We're so excited that you're joining us for this 30-Day Prayer Challenge, and we believe it will be a transformative experience as you deepen your relationship with God.

As you read through the pages of Going Beyond Amen, we trust that you were inspired and equipped to cultivate a more powerful and effective prayer life. Now, as you embark on this 30-day challenge, you'll have the opportunity to put those principles into practice and experience firsthand the incredible ways God moves in response to prayer.

Don't Forget Your Companion!

We encourage you to use the Going Beyond Amen journal companion to enhance your journey. This journal provides a structured framework for daily reflection, prayer, and Scripture meditation, allowing you to track your progress, record your insights, and celebrate answered prayers.

Here are a few reminders as you begin the challenge:

Stay consistent: Set aside dedicated time each day to connect with God through prayer and journaling. Even a few minutes of focused prayer can make a significant difference.

Be open and honest: Pour out your heart to God, sharing your joys, concerns, and requests with complete honesty.

Expect God to move: Approach this challenge with faith and anticipation, believing that God hears your prayers and is eager to work in your life.

We're confident that as you faithfully engage in this 30-Day Prayer Challenge, you'll experience a deeper connection with God, a greater sense of His presence, and a renewed passion for prayer.

Blessings on your journey, Prayer Warrior!

Your Partner In Prayer, Alisa

Meet The Author: Alisa Ladawn Grace

Alisa Ladawn Grace is a multifaceted individual who embodies a life dedicated to love, service, and, most importantly, unwavering reliance on God. As a retired school administrator, author, transformative life coach, and devoted local missionary, Alisa has spent over 30 years spreading the transformative power of God's love in a world often marked by division and uncertainty.

For Alisa, prayer is not just an activity—it is the very rhythm of her existence. Her commitment to fully relying on God through prayer and the guidance of the Holy Spirit has shaped every aspect of her life, from her personal decisions to her work as an author and mentor. This deep connection with God has allowed Alisa to walk through life with a profound sense of peace, purpose, and trust, serving as an example to all who seek to deepen their faith.

In her writings, Alisa encourages others to embark on their own prayer journey, relying on God as their guide and source of strength. Her belief that prayer is the lifeline to God's heart is evident in every word she shares, as she invites her readers to go beyond the simple "amen" and step into a deeper, more transformative relationship with their Creator.

Love's Unconditional Revolution! Unleash and Ignite the Transformative Power of Love

In this powerful book, Alisa explores the practical application of the timeless principles of love found in 1 Corinthians 13. Discover how these principles can revolutionize relationships, work, personal growth, and spirituality. Prepare to be amazed at love's

profound impact on your life when you intentionally choose to live by its tenets
.
Other Works by Alisa Ladawn Grace

Alisa's commitment to nurturing the next generation is evident in her children's books, which promote civic engagement and personal development. Titles like Civic Heroes: Discovering Elections with the Supervisor of Elections, My Civic Adventure: Learning About Voting and Community!, and Unlocking Your Great Potential Within You: A Comprehensive Curriculum Guide to Nurturing Children's Meditation, Executive Functioning Skills, and Good Habits empower young minds to make a positive difference in the world.

One Gives Life, and One Steals Life

In her latest work, One Gives Life and One Steals Life, Alisa delves into the profound impact of our choices on our present lives and the legacy we leave for future generations. Through insightful exploration and a heartfelt call to action, Alisa encourages readers to choose life by aligning their decisions with God's will and teaching the next generation to do the same. This book is a powerful reminder that our choices matter and that we have the power to create a life-giving legacy that will bless generations to come.

Mind Architect: How Your Thoughts Design Your Destiny

In addition to her other transformative works, Alisa Ladawn Grace invites you on a journey of self-discovery and empowerment with Mind Architect: How Your Thoughts Design Your Destiny. This book delves into the profound connection between your thoughts and the reality you create, providing practical tools to harness the power of your mind and manifest the life you desire.

Through her writing and her life, Alisa Ladawn Grace continues to be a shining example of God's transformative power. Her works inspire, uplift, and empower readers to rely on God, embrace love, make life-giving choices, and create a reality that reflects their deepest desires and highest aspirations, all under the guidance of a loving Creator.

www.ingramcontent.com/pod-product-compliance
Lightning Source LLC
Chambersburg PA
CBHW050919160426
43194CB00011B/2470